Use size 20 cotton thread to work up this lovely garden of pineapple motifs combined with shell and picot stitches.

PINEAPPLE DOILIES

*Lovers of thread crochet consistently name the pineapple motif among their all-time favorite styles. This handy little book features the popular symbol of hospitality in **6 exquisite doilies** that will suit anyone's fancy. Ranging from easy to intricate, the **oval, round, hexagon, and square shapes** measure from **12" square to 18" in diameter**. With our **clear instructions, easy-to-follow stitch diagrams, and true-to-life photographs,** you'll find that fashioning your own heirlooms is a truly "fruitful" experience.*

GENERAL INSTRUCTIONS

ABBREVIATIONS

ch(s)	chain(s)
dc	double crochet(s)
dtr	double treble crochet(s)
hdc	half double crochet(s)
FP	Front Post
FPtr	Front Post treble crochet(s)
mm	millimeters
Rnd(s)	Round(s)
sc	single crochet(s)
sp(s)	space(s)
st(s)	stitch(es)
tr	treble crochet(s)
YO	yarn over

★ — work instructions following ★ as many **more** times as indicated in addition to the first time.

† to † **or** ♥ to ♥ — work all instructions from first † to second † **or** from first ♥ to second ♥ **as many** times as specified.

( ) or [ ] — work enclosed instructions **as many** times as specified by the number immediately following **or** work all enclosed instructions in the stitch or space indicated **or** contains explanatory remarks.

colon (:) — the number(s) given after a colon at the end of a row or round denote(s) the number of stitches you should have on that row or round.

©1999 by Leisure Arts, Inc.
P.O. Box 55595, Little Rock, AR 72215

ISBN 1-57486-968-X

GAUGE

Exact gauge is **essential** for proper size. Hook size given in instructions is merely a guide and should never be used without first making a sample swatch of the rounds indicated in the thread and hook specified. Then measure the swatch, counting your stitches and rounds carefully. If your swatch is larger or smaller than specified, **make another, changing hook size to get the correct gauge**. Keep trying until you find the size hook that will give you the specified gauge.

CHAIN

To work a chain stitch, begin with a slip knot on the hook. Bring the yarn **over** hook from back to front, catching the yarn with the hook and turning the hook slightly toward you to keep the yarn from slipping off. Draw the yarn through the slip knot *(Fig. 1)* **(first chain st made, abbreviated ch)**.

Fig. 1

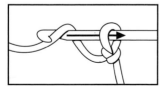

WORKING INTO THE CHAIN

When counting chains, always begin with the first chain from the hook and then count toward the beginning of your foundation chain *(Fig. 2a)*.

Fig. 2a

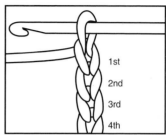

Method 1: Insert hook under top two strands of each chain *(Fig. 2b)*.

Fig. 2b

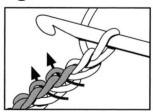

Method 2: Insert hook into back ridge of each chain *(Fig. 2c)*.

Fig. 2c

Method 3: To form a beginning ring, work the specified number of chains and then join to the first chain made with a slip st *(Fig. 2d)*.

Fig. 2d

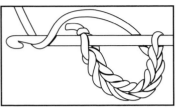

SLIP STITCH

To work a slip stitch, insert hook in st or sp indicated, YO and draw through st and through loop on hook *(Fig. 3)* **(slip stitch made,** *abbreviated slip st)*.

Fig. 3

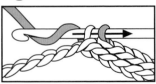

SINGLE CROCHET

Insert hook in st or sp indicated, YO and pull up a loop, YO and draw through both loops on hook *(Fig. 4)* **(single crochet made,** *abbreviated sc)*.

Fig. 4

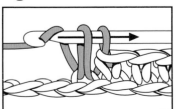

HALF DOUBLE CROCHET

YO, insert hook in st or sp indicated, YO and pull up a loop, YO and draw through all 3 loops on hook *(Fig. 5)* **(half double crochet made,** *abbreviated hdc)*.

Fig. 5

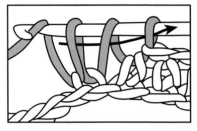

DOUBLE CROCHET

YO, insert hook in st or sp indicated, YO and pull up a loop (3 loops on hook), YO and draw through 2 loops on hook *(Fig. 6a)*, YO and draw through remaining 2 loops on hook *(Fig. 6b)* **(double crochet made,** *abbreviated dc)*.

Fig. 6a

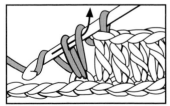

Fig. 6b

TREBLE CROCHET

YO twice, insert hook in st or sp indicated, YO and pull up a loop (4 loops on hook) *(Fig. 7a)*, (YO and draw through 2 loops on hook) 3 times *(Fig. 7b)* (treble crochet made, *abbreviated tr)*.

Fig. 7a

Fig. 7b

DOUBLE TREBLE CROCHET

YO 3 times, insert hook in st or sp indicated, YO and pull up a loop (5 loops on hook) *(Fig. 8a)*, (YO and draw through 2 loops on hook) 4 times *(Fig. 8b)* (double treble crochet made, *abbreviated dtr)*.

Fig. 8a

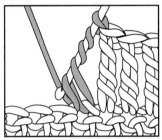

Fig. 8b

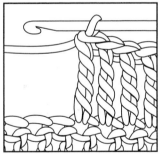

CROCHET TERMINOLOGY	
UNITED STATES	**INTERNATIONAL**
slip stitch (slip st)	= single crochet (sc)
single crochet (sc)	= double crochet (dc)
half double crochet (hdc)	= half treble crochet (htr)
double crochet (dc)	= treble crochet (tr)
treble crochet (tr)	= double treble crochet (dtr)
double treble crochet (dtr)	= triple treble crochet (ttr)
skip	= miss

FREE LOOPS OF A CHAIN

When instructed to work in free loops of a chain, work in loop indicated by arrow *(Fig. 9)*.

Fig. 9

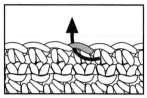

POST STITCH

Work around post of st indicated, inserting hook in direction of arrow *(Fig. 10)*.

Fig. 10

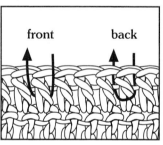

front   back

WORKING IN SIDE OF STITCH

When instructed to work in side of stitch just worked, insert hook as indicated by arrow *(Fig. 11)*.

Fig. 11

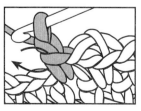

WASHING AND BLOCKING

For a more professional look, pieces should be washed and blocked. Using a mild detergent and warm water and being careful not to rub, twist, or wring, gently squeeze suds through the piece. Rinse several times in cool, clear water. Roll piece in a clean terry towel and gently press out the excess moisture. Lay piece on a flat surface and shape to proper size; where needed, pin in place using rust-proof pins. Allow to dry **completely**.

STEEL CROCHET HOOKS	
UNITED STATES	METRIC (mm)
00	3.50
0	3.25
1	2.75
2	2.25
3	2.10
4	2.00
5	1.90
6	1.80
7	1.65
8	1.50
9	1.40
10	1.30
11	1.10
12	1.00
13	0.85
14	0.75

1. PINEAPPLE BLOSSOM

Shown on Front Cover.

Finished Size:
18" diameter

MATERIALS

Bedspread Weight Cotton Thread (size 10): 350 yards Steel crochet hook, size 8 (1.50 mm) **or** size needed for gauge

GAUGE: Rnds 1-4 = 3"

Note: This Doily may ruffle slightly as you crochet. These ruffles will smooth out when the completed Doily is blocked.

To work treble crochet (abbreviated tr), YO twice, insert hook in sc indicated, YO and pull up a loop (4 loops on hook), (YO and draw through 2 loops on hook) 3 times *(Figs. 7a & b, page 6).*

Ch 12; join with slip st to form a ring.

Rnd 1 (Right side)**:** Ch 1, sc in ring, (ch 6, sc in ring) 5 times, ch 2, tr in first sc to form last loop: 6 loops.

Rnd 2: Ch 1, (sc, ch 3) twice in same loop and in each loop around; join with slip st to first sc: 12 ch-3 sps.

To work Shell, (2 dc, ch 2, 2 dc) in sp indicated.

Rnd 3: Slip st in first ch-3 sp, ch 3 **(counts as first dc, now and throughout),** (dc, ch 2, 2 dc) in same sp, ch 3, dc in next ch-3 sp, ch 3, ★ work Shell in next ch-3 sp, ch 3, dc in next ch-3 sp, ch 3; repeat from ★ around; join with slip st to first dc: 18 sps.

To work beginning Shell, slip st in next dc and in next ch-2 sp, ch 3, (dc, ch 2, 2 dc) in same sp.

To work V-St, (dc, ch 1, dc) in dc indicated.

Rnd 4: Work beginning Shell, ch 3, skip next 2 dc, work V-St in next dc, ch 3, ★ work Shell in next Shell (ch-2 sp), ch 3, skip next 2 dc, work V-St in next dc, ch 3; repeat from ★ around; join with slip st to first dc: 6 V-Sts and 6 Shells.

Rnd 5: Work beginning Shell, ch 3, skip next 2 dc, work V-St in next dc, ch 1, work V-St in next dc, ch 3, ★ work Shell in next Shell, ch 3, skip next 2 dc, work V-St in next dc, ch 1, work V-St in next dc, ch 3; repeat from ★ around; join with slip st to first dc: 12 V-Sts and 6 Shells.

Rnd 6: Work beginning Shell, ch 3, skip next 2 dc, work V-St in next dc, (ch 1, work V-St in next dc) 3 times, ch 3, ★ work Shell in next Shell, ch 3, skip next 2 dc, work V-St in next dc, (ch 1, work V-St in next dc) 3 times, ch 3; repeat from ★ around; join with slip st to first dc: 24 V-Sts and 6 Shells.

Rnd 7: Work beginning Shell, ch 3, skip next 2 dc, work V-St in next dc, (ch 1, work V-St in next dc) 7 times, ch 3, ★ work Shell in next Shell, ch 3, skip next 2 dc, work V-St in next dc, (ch 1, work V-St in next dc) 7 times, ch 3; repeat from ★ around; join with slip st to first dc: 48 V-Sts and 6 Shells.

Rnd 8: Work beginning Shell, ch 3, skip next ch-3 sp, (sc in next ch-1 sp, ch 3) 15 times, ★ work Shell in next Shell, ch 3, skip next ch-3 sp, (sc in next ch-1 sp, ch 3) 15 times; repeat from ★ around; join with slip st to first dc: 102 sps.

Rnd 9: Work beginning Shell, ch 3, skip next ch-3 sp, (sc in next ch-3 sp, ch 3) 14 times, ★ work Shell in next Shell, ch 3, skip next ch-3 sp, (sc in next ch-3 sp, ch 3) 14 times; repeat from ★ around; join with slip st to first dc: 96 sps.

Rnd 10: Work beginning Shell, ch 3, skip next ch-3 sp, (sc in next ch-3 sp, ch 3) 13 times, ★ work Shell in next Shell, ch 3, skip next ch-3 sp, (sc in next ch-3 sp, ch 3) 13 times; repeat from ★ around; join with slip st to first dc: 90 sps.

Rnd 11: Work beginning Shell, ch 3, skip next ch-3 sp, (sc in next ch-3 sp, ch 3) 12 times, ★ work Shell in next Shell, ch 3, skip next ch-3 sp, (sc in next ch-3 sp, ch 3) 12 times; repeat from ★ around; join with slip st to first dc: 84 sps.

Rnd 12: Work beginning Shell, ch 3, skip next ch-3 sp, (sc in next ch-3 sp, ch 3) 11 times, ★ work Shell in next Shell, ch 3, skip next ch-3 sp, (sc in next ch-3 sp, ch 3) 11 times; repeat from ★ around; join with slip st to first dc: 78 sps.

Rnd 13: Work beginning Shell, ch 3, work Shell in same sp, ch 3, skip next ch-3 sp, (sc in next ch-3 sp, ch 3) 10 times, ★ (work Shell, ch 3) twice in next Shell, skip next ch-3 sp, (sc in next ch-3 sp, ch 3) 10 times; repeat from ★ around; join with slip st to first dc: 84 sps.

Rnd 14: Work beginning Shell, ch 3, dc in next ch-3 sp, ch 3, work Shell in next Shell, ch 3, skip next ch-3 sp, (sc in next ch-3 sp, ch 3) 9 times, ★ work Shell in next Shell, ch 3, dc in next ch-3 sp, ch 3, work Shell in next Shell, ch 3, skip next ch-3 sp, (sc in next ch-3 sp, ch 3) 9 times; repeat from ★ around; join with slip st to first dc.

Rnd 15: Work beginning Shell, ch 3, skip next 2 dc, work V-St in next dc, ch 3, work Shell in next Shell, ch 3, skip next ch-3 sp, (sc in next ch-3 sp, ch 3) 8 times, ★ work Shell in next Shell, ch 3, skip next 2 dc, work V-St in next dc, ch 3, work Shell in next Shell, ch 3, skip next ch-3 sp, (sc in next ch-3 sp, ch 3) 8 times; repeat from ★ around; join with slip st to first dc.

Rnd 16: Work beginning Shell, ch 3, skip next 2 dc, work V-St in next dc, ch 1, work V-St in next dc, ch 3, work Shell in next Shell, ch 3, skip next ch-3 sp, (sc in next ch-3 sp, ch 3) 7 times, ★ work Shell in next Shell, ch 3, skip next 2 dc, work V-St in next dc, ch 1, work V-St in next dc, ch 3, work Shell in next Shell, ch 3, skip next ch-3 sp, (sc in next ch-3 sp, ch 3) 7 times; repeat from ★ around; join with slip st to first dc: 90 sps.

Rnd 17: Work beginning Shell, ch 3, skip next 2 dc, work V-St in next dc, (ch 1, work V-St in next dc) 3 times, ch 3, work Shell in next Shell, ch 3, skip next ch-3 sp, (sc in next ch-3 sp, ch 3) 6 times, ★ work Shell in next Shell, ch 3, skip next 2 dc, work V-St in next dc, (ch 1, work V-St in next dc) 3 times, ch 3, work Shell in next Shell, ch 3, skip next ch-3 sp, (sc in next ch-3 sp, ch 3) 6 times; repeat from ★ around; join with slip st to first dc: 108 sps.

Rnd 18: Work beginning Shell, ch 2, 2 dc in same sp, ch 3, skip next ch-3 sp, (sc in next ch-1 sp, ch 3) 7 times, (work Shell, ch 2, 2 dc) in next Shell, ch 3, skip next ch-3 sp, (sc in next ch-3 sp, ch 3) 5 times, ★ (work Shell, ch 2, 2 dc) in next Shell, ch 3, skip next ch-3 sp, (sc in next ch-1 sp, ch 3) 7 times, (work Shell, ch 2, 2 dc) in next Shell, ch 3, skip next ch-3 sp, (sc in next ch-3 sp, ch 3) 5 times; repeat from ★ around; join with slip st to first dc.

Rnd 19: Work beginning Shell, work Shell in next ch-2 sp, ch 3, skip next ch-3 sp, (sc in next ch-3 sp, ch 3) 6 times, skip next ch-3 sp, work Shell in each of next 2 ch-2 sps, ch 3, skip next ch-3 sp, (sc in next ch-3 sp, ch 3) 4 times, skip next ch-3 sp, ★ work Shell in each of next 2 ch-2 sps, ch 3, skip next ch-3 sp, (sc in next ch-3 sp, ch 3) 6 times, skip next ch-3 sp, work Shell in each of next 2 ch-2 sps, ch 3, skip next ch-3 sp, (sc in next ch-3 sp, ch 3) 4 times, skip next ch-3 sp; repeat from ★ around; join with slip st to first dc: 96 sps.

Rnd 20: Work beginning Shell, ch 2, 2 dc in same sp, (work Shell, ch 2, 2 dc) in next Shell, ch 3, skip next ch-3 sp, (sc in next ch-3 sp, ch 3) 5 times, (work Shell, ch 2, 2 dc) in each of next 2 Shells, ch 3, skip next ch-3 sp, (sc in next ch-3 sp, ch 3) 3 times, ★ (work Shell, ch 2, 2 dc) in each of next 2 Shells, ch 3, skip next ch-3 sp, (sc in next ch-3 sp, ch 3) 5 times, (work Shell, ch 2, 2 dc) in each of next 2 Shells, ch 3, skip next ch-3 sp, (sc in next ch-3 sp, ch 3) 3 times; repeat from ★ around; join with slip st to first dc: 108 sps.

Rnd 21: Work beginning Shell, work Shell in each of next 3 ch-2 sps, ch 3, skip next ch-3 sp, (sc in next ch-3 sp, ch 3) 4 times, skip next ch-3 sp, work Shell in each of next 4 ch-2 sps, ch 3, skip next ch-3 sp, (sc in next ch-3 sp, ch 3) twice, skip next ch-3 sp, ★ work Shell in each of next 4 ch-2 sps, ch 3, skip next ch-3 sp, (sc in next ch-3 sp, ch 3) 4 times, skip next ch-3 sp, work Shell in each of next 4 ch-2 sps, ch 3, skip next ch-3 sp, (sc in next ch-3 sp, ch 3) twice, skip next ch-3 sp; repeat from ★ around; join with slip st to first dc: 48 Shells.

Rnd 22: Work beginning Shell, ch 2, 2 dc in same sp, (work Shell, ch 2, 2 dc) in each of next 3 Shells, ch 3, skip next ch-3 sp, (sc in next ch-3 sp, ch 3) 3 times, (work Shell, ch 2, 2 dc) in each of next 4 Shells, ch 3, skip next ch-3 sp, sc in next ch-3 sp, ch 3, ★ (work Shell, ch 2, 2 dc) in each of next 4 Shells, ch 3, skip next ch-3 sp, (sc in next ch-3 sp, ch 3) 3 times, (work Shell, ch 2, 2 dc) in each of next

4 Shells, ch 3, skip next ch-3 sp, sc in next ch-3 sp, ch 3; repeat from ★ around; join with slip st to first dc: 132 sps.

Rnd 23: Work beginning Shell, work Shell in each of next 7 ch-2 sps, ch 3, skip next ch-3 sp, (sc in next ch-3 sp, ch 3) twice, skip next ch-3 sp, work Shell in each of next 8 ch-2 sps, skip next 2 ch-3 sps, ★ work Shell in each of next 8 ch-2 sps, ch 3, skip next ch-3 sp, (sc in next ch-3 sp, ch 3) twice, skip next ch-3 sp, work Shell in each of next 8 ch-2 sps, skip next 2 ch-3 sps; repeat from ★ around; join with slip st to first dc: 96 Shells.

Rnd 24: Work beginning Shell, work Shell in each of next 7 Shells, ch 3, skip next ch-3 sp, sc in next ch-3 sp, ch 3, ★ work Shell in each of next 16 Shells, ch 3, skip next ch-3 sp, sc in next ch-3 sp, ch 3; repeat from ★ 4 times **more**, work Shell in each of last 8 Shells; join with slip st to first dc.

To work Picot, ch 6, slip st in third ch from hook.

Rnd 25: Slip st in next dc and in next ch-2 sp, ch 1, sc in same sp, work Picot, ch 3, ★ sc in next Shell, work Picot, ch 3; repeat from ★ around; join with slip st to first sc, finish off.

See Washing and Blocking, page 7.

Design by Delsie Rhoades.

2. PINEAPPLE GARDEN

Shown on page 2.

Finished Size:
11½" x 18½"

MATERIALS
Cotton Crochet Thread (size 20): 365 yards
Steel crochet hook, size 9 (1.40 mm) **or** size needed for gauge
GAUGE: Rnds 1-3 = 1½" x 8½"

Ch 96.

Rnd 1 (Right side)**:** 11 Dc in fourth ch from hook **(3 skipped chs count as first dc, now and throughout)**, † skip next 3 chs, sc in next ch, (ch 5, skip next 4 chs, sc in next ch) 3 times, ★ skip next 3 chs, 8 dc in next ch, skip next 3 chs, sc in next ch, (ch 5, skip next 4 chs, sc in next ch) 3 times; repeat from ★ 2 times **more**, skip next 3 chs †, 12 dc in last ch; working in free loops of beginning ch **(Fig. 9, page 7)**, repeat from † to † once; join with slip st to first dc: 72 dc and 24 loops.

Note: Mark last round as **right** side.

Rnd 2: Ch 6 **(counts as first dc plus ch 3)**, dc in next dc, (ch 3, dc in next dc) 10 times, † sc in next loop, (ch 5, sc in next loop) twice, ★ dc in next dc, (ch 1, dc in next dc) 7 times, sc in next loop, (ch 5, sc in next loop) twice; repeat from ★ 2 times **more** †, dc in next dc, (ch 3, dc in next dc) 11 times,

repeat from † to † once; join with slip st to first dc: 64 sps and 16 loops.

To work beginning Cluster, slip st in first ch-3 sp, ch 2, ★ YO, insert hook in same sp, YO and pull up a loop, YO and draw through 2 loops on hook; repeat from ★ once **more**, YO and draw through all 3 loops on hook.

To work Cluster *(uses one sp)*, ★ YO, insert hook in sp indicated, YO and pull up a loop, YO and draw through 2 loops on hook; repeat from ★ 2 times **more**, YO and draw through all 4 loops on hook.

Rnd 3: Work beginning Cluster, † (ch 3, work Cluster in next ch-3 sp) 10 times, sc in next loop, ch 5, sc in next loop, ★ work Cluster in next ch-1 sp, (ch 3, work Cluster in next ch-1 sp) 6 times, sc in next loop, ch 5, sc in next loop; repeat from ★ 2 times **more** †, work Cluster in next ch-3 sp, repeat from † to † once; join with slip st to top of beginning Cluster: 64 Clusters.

To work Large Picot, ch 4, slip st in side of last sc made **(Fig. 11, page 7)**.

Rnd 4: Slip st in first ch-3 sp, ch 1, (2 sc, work Large Picot, 2 sc) in same sp, ch 2, 2 sc in next ch-3 sp, work Large Picot, place marker around Picot just made for joining placement, 2 sc in same sp, ch 2, [(2 sc, work Large Picot, 2 sc) in next ch-3 sp, ch 2] 8 times, † (sc, work Large Picot, sc) in next loop, ch 2, ★ [(2 sc, work Large Picot, 2 sc) in next ch-3 sp, ch 2] 6 times, (sc, work Large Picot, sc) in next loop, ch 2; repeat from ★ 2 times **more** †, [(2 sc, work Large Picot, 2 sc) in next ch-3 sp, ch 2] 10 times, repeat from † to † once; join with slip st to first sc, finish off: 64 Large Picots.

To work 3-dc Shell, (3 dc, ch 3, 3 dc) in sp or loop indicated.

To work dtr Cluster (uses next 3 Picots), ★ YO 3 times, insert hook in **next** Picot, YO and pull up a loop, (YO and draw through 2 loops on hook) 3 times; repeat from ★ 2 times **more**, YO and draw through all 4 loops on hook.

To work treble crochet (abbreviated tr), YO twice, insert hook in st, sp, or loop indicated, YO and pull up a loop (4 loops on hook), (YO and draw through 2 loops on hook) 3 times *(Figs. 7a & b, page 6)*.

Rnd 5: Ch 4, (2 dc, ch 3, 3 dc) in fourth ch from hook, place marker around last dc made for st placement, ch 3; with **right** side facing, dc in marked Picot, ♥ ch 3, **turn**; work 3-dc Shell in next Shell (ch-3 sp), ch 7, **turn**; work 3-dc Shell in next Shell, ch 3, dc in next Picot, ch 3, **turn**; work 3-dc Shell in next Shell, ch 7, **turn**; work 3-dc Shell in next Shell, ch 3, ★ dc in next Picot, ch 3, **turn**; work 3-dc Shell in next Shell, ch 7, **turn**; work 3-dc Shell in next Shell, ch 3, dc in same Picot, ch 3, **turn**; work 3-dc Shell in next Shell, ch 7, **turn**; work 3-dc Shell in next Shell, ch 3; repeat from ★ 3 times **more**, [dc in next Picot, ch 3, **turn**; work 3-dc Shell in next Shell, ch 7, **turn**; work 3-dc Shell in next Shell, ch 3] twice, work dtr Cluster, † ch 3, **turn**; work 3-dc Shell in next Shell, ch 7, **turn**; work 3-dc Shell in next Shell, ch 3, dc in next Picot, ch 3, **turn**; work 3-dc Shell in next Shell, ch 7, **turn**; work 3-dc Shell in next Shell, ch 3, skip next Picot, dc in next ch-2 sp, ch 3, **turn**; work 3-dc Shell in next Shell, ch 7, **turn**; work 3-dc Shell in next Shell, ch 3, skip next Picot, dc in next Picot, ch 3, **turn**; work 3-dc Shell in next Shell, ch 7, **turn**; work 3-dc Shell in next Shell, ch 3, work dtr Cluster †, repeat from † to † 2 times **more** ♥, ch 3, **turn**; work 3-dc Shell in next Shell, ch 7, **turn**; work 3-dc Shell in next Shell, ch 3, dc in next Picot, repeat from ♥ to ♥ once, ch 3, **turn**; 3 dc in next Shell, slip st in base of marked dc, ch 1, skip next 4 dc on first Shell, slip st in base of next dc, 3 dc in same sp on last Shell, ch 3, **turn**; tr in top of first dc to form last loop: 50 loops.

Rnd 6: Ch 7 **(counts as first tr plus ch 3)**, tr in same loop, † [ch 7, (tr, ch 3, tr) in next loop] 12 times †, (ch 3, tr) twice in each of next 13 loops, repeat from † to † once, ch 3, (tr, ch 3) twice in each of last 12 loops; join with slip st to first tr: 76 ch-3 sps and 24 loops.

To work 2-dc Shell, (2 dc, ch 2, 2 dc) in ch or sp indicated.

Rnd 7: Slip st in first ch-3 sp, ch 3 **(counts as first dc, now and throughout)**, (dc, ch 2, 2 dc) in same sp, † (work 2-dc Shell in center ch of next loop, work 2-dc Shell in next ch-3 sp) 12 times †, (skip next ch-3 sp, work 2-dc Shell in next ch-3 sp) 13 times, repeat from † to † once, skip next ch-3 sp, (work 2-dc Shell in next ch-3 sp, skip next ch-3 sp) 12 times; join with slip st to first dc: 74 Shells.

To work beginning 2-dc Shell, slip st in next dc and in next ch-2 sp, ch 3, (dc, ch 2, 2 dc) in same sp.

Rnds 8 and 9: Work beginning 2-dc Shell, work 2-dc Shell in each Shell (ch-2 sp) around; join with slip st to first dc.

Rnd 10: Slip st in next dc and in next ch-2 sp, ch 1, 3 sc in same sp, ch 4, slip st in second ch from hook, ch 2, sc in next Shell, ch 11, sc in tenth ch from hook, place marker around loop just made for joining placement, sc in next ch and in same Shell, ch 4, slip st in second ch from hook, ch 2, [sc in next Shell, ch 11, sc in tenth ch from hook, sc in next ch and in same Shell, ch 4, slip st in second ch from hook, ch 2] 22 times, 3 sc in next Shell, ch 12, sc in tenth ch from hook and in next ch, ch 1, 3 sc in next Shell, ch 4, slip st in second ch from hook, ch 2, ★ sc in next Shell, ch 11, sc in tenth ch from hook, sc in next ch and in same Shell, ch 4, slip st in second ch from hook, ch 2, 3 sc in next Shell, ch 12, sc in tenth ch from hook and in next ch, ch 1, 3 sc in next Shell, ch 4, slip st in second ch from hook, ch 2; repeat from ★ 3 times **more**, [sc in next Shell, ch 11, sc in tenth ch from hook, sc in next ch and in same Shell, ch 4, slip st in second ch from hook, ch 2] 23 times, 3 sc in next Shell, ch 12, sc in tenth ch from hook and in next ch, ch 1, † 3 sc in next Shell, ch 4, slip st in second ch from hook, ch 2, sc in next Shell, ch 11, sc in tenth ch from hook, sc in next ch and in same Shell, ch 4, slip st in second ch from hook, ch 2, 3 sc in next Shell, ch 12, sc in tenth ch from hook and in next ch, ch 1 †, repeat from † to † 3 times **more**; join with slip st to first sc, finish off: 64 loops.

Rnd 11: With **right** side facing, join thread with slip st in marked loop; ch 3, (2 dc, ch 3, 3 dc) in same loop, † (ch 3, sc in center ch of next loop, ch 3, work 3-dc Shell in next loop) 11 times †, (ch 5, sc in center ch of next loop, ch 5, work 3-dc Shell in next loop) 5 times, repeat from † to † once, ch 5, sc in center ch of next loop, ch 5, (work 3-dc Shell in next loop, ch 5, sc in center ch of next loop, ch 5) 4 times; join with slip st to first dc: 32 Shells.

To work beginning 3-dc Shell, slip st in next 2 dc and in next ch-3 sp, ch 3, (2 dc, ch 3, 3 dc) in same sp.

To work V-St, (dc, ch 3, dc) in st or sp indicated.

Rnd 12: Work beginning 3-dc Shell, † (ch 3, work V-St in next sc, ch 3, work 3-dc Shell in next Shell) 11 times †, (ch 4, work V-St in next sc, ch 4, work 3-dc Shell in next Shell) 5 times, repeat from † to † once, ch 4, work V-St in next sc, ch 4, (work 3-dc Shell in next Shell, ch 4, work V-St in next sc, ch 4) 4 times; join with slip st to first dc.

Rnd 13: Work beginning 3-dc Shell, † [ch 3, work V-St in next V-St (ch-3 sp), ch 3, work 3-dc Shell in next Shell] 11 times †, (ch 4, work V-St in next V-St, ch 4, work 3-dc Shell in next Shell) 5 times, repeat from † to † once, ch 4, work V-St in next V-St, ch 4, (work 3-dc Shell in next Shell, ch 4, work V-St in next V-St, ch 4) 4 times; join with slip st to first dc.

Rnd 14: Work beginning 3-dc Shell, † (ch 2, skip next ch-3 sp, dc in next dc, 5 dc in next ch-3 sp, dc in next dc, ch 2, work 3-dc Shell in next Shell) 11 times †, (ch 3, skip next ch-4 sp, dc in next dc, 5 dc in next ch-3 sp, dc in next dc, ch 3, work 3-dc Shell in next Shell) 5 times, repeat from † to † once, ch 3, skip next ch-4 sp, dc in next dc, 5 dc in next ch-3 sp, dc in next dc, ch 3, (work 3-dc Shell in next Shell, ch 3, skip next ch-4 sp, dc in next dc, 5 dc in next ch-3 sp, dc in next dc, ch 3) 4 times; join with slip st to first dc: 416 dc.

Rnd 15: Work beginning 3-dc Shell, ch 1, skip next ch-2 sp, (dc in next dc, ch 1) 7 times, ★ work 3-dc Shell in next Shell, ch 1, skip next sp, (dc in next dc, ch 1) 7 times; repeat from ★ around; join with slip st to first dc.

Rnd 16: Work beginning 3-dc Shell, ch 2, skip next ch-1 sp, (sc in next ch-1 sp, ch 2) 6 times, ★ work 3-dc Shell in next Shell, ch 2, skip next ch-1 sp, (sc in next ch-1 sp, ch 2) 6 times; repeat from ★ around; join with slip st to first dc: 256 sps.

Rnd 17: Work beginning 3-dc Shell, ch 3, skip next ch-2 sp, sc in next ch-2 sp, (ch 2, sc in next ch-2 sp) 4 times, ch 3, ★ work 3-dc Shell in next Shell, ch 3, skip next ch-2 sp, sc in next ch-2 sp, (ch 2, sc in next ch-2 sp) 4 times, ch 3; repeat from ★ around; join with slip st to first dc: 224 sps.

Rnd 5: Ch 3, 2 dc in same sp, ch 3, skip next ch-3 sp, dc in next dc, (ch 1, dc in next dc) 8 times, ch 3, ★ work Shell in next Shell, ch 3, skip next ch-3 sp, dc in next dc, (ch 1, dc in next dc) 8 times, ch 3; repeat from ★ around, 3 dc in same sp as first dc, ch 2, sc in first dc to form last sp.

Rnd 6: Ch 3, 2 dc in same sp, ch 3, skip next ch-3 sp, dc in next dc, (ch 2, dc in next dc) 8 times, ch 3, ★ work Shell in next Shell, ch 3, skip next ch-3 sp, dc in next dc, (ch 2, dc in next dc) 8 times, ch 3; repeat from ★ around, 3 dc in same sp as first dc, ch 2, sc in first dc to form last sp.

Rnd 7: Ch 3, 2 dc in same sp, ch 3, ★ † skip next ch-3 sp, sc in next ch-2 sp, (ch 5, sc in next ch-2 sp) 7 times, ch 3 †, (3 dc, ch 3) 3 times in next Shell; repeat from ★ 2 times **more**, then repeat from † to † once, work Shell in same sp as first dc, ch 2, sc in first dc to form last sp.

Rnd 8: Ch 3, 2 dc in same sp, ★ † ch 3, skip next ch-3 sp, sc next ch-5 sp, (ch 5, sc in next ch-5 sp) 6 times, ch 3, skip next ch-3 sp, work Shell in next ch-3 sp, ch 5 †, work Shell in next ch-3 sp; repeat from ★ 2 times **more**, then repeat from † to † once, 3 dc in same sp as first dc, ch 2, sc in first dc to form last sp.

To work Picot, ch 3, slip st in side of st just worked *(Fig. 11, page 7)*.

Rnd 9: Ch 3, 2 dc in same sp, ★ † ch 3, skip next ch-3 sp, sc in next ch-5 sp, (ch 5, sc in next ch-5 sp) 5 times, ch 3, work Shell in next Shell, ch 3, (sc, work Picot, ch 5, sc, work Picot) in next ch-5 sp, ch 3 †, work Shell in next Shell; repeat from ★ 2 times **more**, then repeat from † to † once, 3 dc in same sp as first dc, ch 2, sc in first dc to form last sp.

Rnd 10: Ch 3, 2 dc in same sp, ★ † ch 3, skip next ch-3 sp, sc in next ch-5 sp, (ch 5, sc in next ch-5 sp) 4 times, ch 3, work Shell in next Shell, ch 5, (sc, work Picot, ch 5, sc, work Picot) in next ch-5 sp, ch 5 †, work Shell in next Shell; repeat from ★ 2 times **more**, then repeat from † to † once, 3 dc in same sp a first dc, ch 2, sc in first dc to form last sp.

Rnd 11: Ch 3, 2 dc in same sp, ★ † ch 3, skip next ch-3 sp, sc in next ch-5 sp, (ch 5, sc in next ch-5 sp) 3 times, ch 3, work Shell in next Shell, ch 7, skip next ch-5 sp, (sc, work Picot, ch 5, sc, work Picot) in next ch-5 sp, ch 7 †, work Shell in next Shell; repeat from ★ 2 times **more**, then repeat from † to † once, 3 dc in same sp as first dc, ch 2, sc in first dc to form last sp.

Rnd 12: Ch 3, 2 dc in same sp, ★ † ch 3, skip next ch-3 sp, sc in next ch-5 sp, (ch 5, sc in next ch-5 sp) twice, ch 3, work Shell in next Shell, ch 9, skip next loop, dc in next ch-5 sp, (work Picot, ch 1, dc) 5 times in same sp, work Picot, ch 9 †, work Shell in next Shell; repeat from ★ 2 times **more**, then repeat from † to † once, 3 dc in same sp as first dc, ch 2, sc in first dc to form last sp.

Rnd 13: Ch 3, 2 dc in same sp, ch 3, ★ † skip next ch-3 sp, sc in next ch-5 sp, ch 5, sc in next ch-5 sp, (ch 3, 3 dc) 3 times in next Shell, ch 9, skip next loop, (dc in next ch-1 sp, work Picot, ch 3) twice, (dc, work Picot, ch 5, dc, work Picot) in next ch-1 sp, (ch 3, dc in next ch-1 sp, work Picot) twice, ch 9 †, (3 dc, ch 3) 3 times in next Shell; repeat from ★ 2 times **more**, then repeat from † to † once, work Shell in same sp as first dc, ch 2, sc in first dc to form last sp.

Rnd 14: Ch 3, 2 dc in same sp, ★ † ch 4, skip next ch-3 sp, sc in next ch-5 sp, ch 4, skip next ch-3 sp, work Shell in next ch-3 sp, ch 3, work Shell in next ch-3 sp, ch 9, skip next loop, (dc in next ch-3 sp, work Picot, ch 5) twice, (dc, work Picot, ch 5, dc, work Picot) in next ch-5 sp, (ch 5, dc in next ch-3 sp, work Picot) twice, ch 9, skip next loop, work Shell in next ch-3 sp, ch 3 †, work Shell in next ch-3 sp; repeat from ★ 2 times **more**, then repeat from † to † once, 3 dc in same sp as first dc, ch 2, sc in first dc to form last sp.

Rnd 15: Ch 3, 2 dc in same sp, ★ † ch 4, sc in next sc, ch 4, work Shell in next Shell, ch 3, dc in next ch-3 sp, ch 3, work Shell in next Shell, ch 9, skip next loop, (dc in next ch-5 sp, work Picot, ch 5) twice, (dc, work Picot, ch 5, dc, work Picot) in next ch-5 sp, (ch 5, dc in next ch-5 sp, work Picot) twice, ch 9, work Shell in next Shell, ch 3, dc in next ch-3 sp, ch 3 †, work Shell in next Shell; repeat from ★ 2 times **more**, then repeat from † to † once, 3 dc in same sp as first dc, ch 2, sc in first dc to form last sp.

Rnd 16: Ch 3, 2 dc in same sp, ★ † skip next 2 ch-4 sps, work Shell in next Shell, ch 3, (dc in next ch-3 sp, ch 3) twice, work Shell in next Shell, ch 9, skip next loop, (dc in next ch-5 sp, work Picot, ch 5) twice, (dc, work Picot, ch 5, dc, work Picot) in next ch-5 sp, (ch 5, dc in next ch-5 sp, work Picot) twice, ch 9, work Shell in next Shell, ch 3, (dc in next ch-3 sp, ch 3) twice †, work Shell in next Shell; repeat from ★ 2 times **more**, then repeat from † to † once, 3 dc in same sp as first dc, ch 2, sc in first dc to form last sp.

To decrease *(uses next 2 Shells)*, ★ YO twice, insert hook in **next** Shell, YO and pull up a loop, (YO and draw through 2 loops on hook) twice, repeat from ★ once **more**, YO and draw through all 3 loops on hook **(counts as one tr)**.

Rnd 17: Ch 3, tr in next Shell, ★ † ch 3, skip next ch-3 sp, (tr in next dc, ch 3) twice, tr in next Shell, ch 3, tr in third ch of next loop, ch 3, skip next 3 chs, tr in next ch, (ch 3, tr in center ch of next ch-5 sp) 3 times, (ch 3, tr) 3 times in same st, (ch 3, tr in center ch of next ch-5 sp) twice, ch 3, tr in third ch of next loop, ch 3, skip next 3 chs, tr in next ch, ch 3, tr in next Shell, (ch 3, tr in next dc) twice, ch 3 †, decrease; repeat from ★ 2 times **more**, then repeat from † to † once, skip beginning ch-3 and join with slip st to first tr.

Rnd 18: Ch 1, sc in same st, 4 sc in next ch-3 sp, (sc in next tr, 4 sc in next ch-3 sp) around; join with slip st to first sc.

Rnd 19: Ch 1, sc in same st, (ch 5, skip next 4 sc, sc in next sc) around to last 4 sc, ch 4, skip last 4 sc, sc in first sc to form last sp: 76 sps.

Rnd 20: Ch 5, ★ (4 dc in next ch-5 sp, ch 2) across to next corner ch-5 sp, (4 dc, ch 2) twice in corner ch-5 sp; repeat from ★ 3 times **more**, (4 dc in next ch-5 sp, ch 2) across, 3 dc in same sp as beginning ch-5; join with slip st to third ch of beginning ch-5.

Rnd 21: Ch 1, ★ † sc in next ch-2 sp and in next dc, ch 3, skip next dc, dc in next dc, work Picot, ch 3 †, repeat from † to † across to next corner ch-2 sp, (sc, ch 3, dc) in corner ch-2 sp, work Picot, ch 3, sc in next dc, ch 3, skip next dc, dc in next dc, work Picot, ch 3; repeat from ★ 3 times **more**, then repeat from † to † across; join with slip st to first sc, finish off.

See Washing and Blocking, page 7.

Design by Dot Drake.

4. PINEAPPLE FANFARE

Shown on page 33.

Finished Size:
14" diameter

MATERIALS
Bedspread Weight Cotton Thread (size 10): 195 yards
Steel crochet hook, size 3 (2.10 mm) **or** size needed for gauge
GAUGE: Rnds 1-4 = 2¼"

Ch 5; join with slip st to form a ring.

Rnd 1 (Right side)**:** Ch 1, sc in ring, (ch 3, sc in ring) 10 times, ch 1, hdc in first sc to form last sp: 11 sps.

Rnds 2 and 3: Ch 1, sc in same sp, (ch 3, sc in next ch-3 sp) around, ch 1, hdc in first sc to form last sp.

***To work Cluster** (uses one sp),* ★ YO, insert hook in sp indicated, YO and pull up a loop, YO and draw through 2 loops on hook; repeat from ★ 4 times **more**, YO and draw through all 6 loops on hook.

Rnd 4: Ch 2, (YO, insert hook in same sp, YO and pull up a loop, YO and draw through 2 loops on hook) 4 times, YO and draw through all 5 loops on hook **(beginning Cluster made)**, ch 2, work Cluster in same sp, (ch 2, work Cluster) twice in each ch-3 sp around, ch 1, sc in top of beginning Cluster to form last sp: 22 Clusters.

Rnd 5: Ch 1, sc in same sp, ch 12, skip next ch-2 sp, ★ sc in next ch-2 sp, ch 12, skip next ch-2 sp; repeat from ★ around; join with slip st to first sc: 11 loops.

Rnd 6: Slip st in next 5 chs, ch 3 **(counts as first dc, now and throughout)**, (dc, ch 2, 2 dc) in same loop, ch 6, ★ (2 dc, ch 2, 2 dc) in next loop, ch 6; repeat from ★ around; join with slip st to first dc: 44 dc.

Rnd 7: Ch 3, dc in next dc, ch 3, (dc, ch 2, dc) in next ch-2 sp, ch 3, dc in next 2 dc, ch 3, sc in next loop, ch 3, ★ dc in next 2 dc, ch 3, (dc, ch 2, dc) in next ch-2 sp, ch 3, dc in next 2 dc, ch 3, sc in next loop, ch 3; repeat from ★ around; join with slip st to first dc: 55 sps.

Rnd 8: Ch 3, dc in next dc, ch 3, skip next ch-3 sp, dc in next ch-2 sp, (ch 1, dc in same sp) 4 times, ch 3, skip next ch-3 sp, dc in next 2 dc, ★ skip next 2 ch-3 sps, dc in next 2 dc, ch 3, skip next ch-3 sp, dc in next ch-2 sp, (ch 1, dc in same sp) 4 times, ch 3, skip next ch-3 sp, dc in next 2 dc; repeat from ★ around; join with slip st to first dc: 66 sps.

Rnd 9: Ch 3, dc in next dc, ch 3, skip next ch-3 sp, (sc in next ch-1 sp, ch 3) 4 times, skip next ch-3 sp, ★ (dc in next 2 dc, ch 3) twice, skip next ch-3 sp, (sc in next ch-1 sp, ch 3) 4 times, skip next ch-3 sp; repeat from ★ around to last 2 dc, dc in last 2 dc, ch 3; join with slip st to first dc.

Rnd 10: Ch 3, dc in next dc, ch 3, skip next ch-3 sp, (sc in next ch-3 sp, ch 3) 3 times, dc in next 2 dc, ch 3, sc in next ch-3 sp, ch 3, ★ dc in next 2 dc, ch 3, skip next ch-3 sp, (sc in next ch-3 sp, ch 3) 3 times, dc in next 2 dc, ch 3, sc in next ch-3 sp, ch 3; repeat from ★ around; join with slip st to first dc.

Rnd 11: Ch 3, dc in next dc, ch 3, skip next ch-3 sp, (sc in next ch-3 sp, ch 3) twice, dc in next 2 dc, ch 3, (sc in next ch-3 sp, ch 3) twice, ★ dc in next 2 dc, ch 3, skip next ch-3 sp, (sc in next ch-3 sp, ch 3) twice, dc in next 2 dc, ch 3, (sc in next ch-3 sp, ch 3) twice; repeat from ★ around; join with slip st to first dc.

Rnd 12: Ch 3, dc in next dc, ch 3, skip next ch-3 sp, sc in next ch-3 sp, ch 3, dc in next 2 dc, ch 3, (sc in next ch-3 sp, ch 3) 3 times, ★ dc in next 2 dc, ch 3, skip next ch-3 sp, sc in next ch-3 sp, ch 3, dc in next 2 dc, ch 3, (sc in next ch-3 sp, ch 3) 3 times; repeat from ★ around; join with slip st to first dc.

Rnd 13: Ch 3, dc in next dc, skip next 2 ch-3 sps, dc in next 2 dc, ch 3, (sc in next ch-3 sp, ch 3) 4 times, ★ dc in next 2 dc, skip next 2 ch-3 sps, dc in next 2 dc, ch 3, (sc in next ch-3 sp, ch 3) 4 times; repeat from ★ around; join with slip st to first dc: 55 ch-3 sps.

To work decrease *(uses next 4 dc)*, ★ YO, insert hook in **next** dc, YO and pull up a loop, YO and draw through 2 loops on hook; repeat from ★ 3 times **more**, YO and draw through all 5 loops on hook.

Rnd 14: Ch 2, (YO, insert hook in **next** dc, YO and pull up a loop, YO and draw through 2 loops on hook) 3 times, YO and draw through all 4 loops on hook **(beginning decrease made)**, ch 3, (sc in next ch-3 sp, ch 3) 5 times, ★ decrease, ch 3, (sc in next ch-3 sp, ch 3) 5 times; repeat from ★ around; join with

slip st to top of beginning decrease: 66 ch-3 sps.

Rnd 15: Slip st in next ch, ch 1, sc in same sp, (ch 3, sc in next ch-3 sp) twice, ch 6, ★ sc in next ch-3 sp, (ch 3, sc in next ch-3 sp) twice, ch 6; repeat from ★ around; join with slip st to first sc: 44 ch-3 sps and 22 loops.

Rnd 16: Slip st in next ch, ch 1, sc in same sp, ch 3, sc in next ch-3 sp, ch 3, (sc, ch 3) twice in next loop, ★ (sc in next ch-3 sp, ch 3) twice, (sc, ch 3) twice in next loop; repeat from ★ around; join with slip st to first sc: 88 ch-3 sps.

Rnd 17: Slip st in next ch, ch 1, sc in same sp, ch 3, skip next ch-3 sp, dc in next ch-3 sp, (ch 1, dc in same sp) 5 times, ch 3, ★ skip next ch-3 sp, (sc in next ch-3 sp, ch 3) 5 times, skip next ch-3 sp, dc in next ch-3 sp, (ch 1, dc in same sp) 5 times, ch 3; repeat from ★ around to last 5 ch-3 sps, skip next ch-3 sp, sc in next ch-3 sp, (ch 3, sc in next ch-3 sp) 3 times, ch 1, hdc in first sc to form last sp: 121 sps.

Rnd 18: Ch 1, sc in same sp, ch 3, dc in next dc, (ch 2, dc in next dc) 5 times, ch 3, ★ skip next ch-3 sp, (sc in next ch-3 sp, ch 3) 4 times, dc in next dc, (ch 2, dc in next dc) 5 times, ch 3; repeat from ★ around to last 4 ch-3 sps, skip next ch-3 sp, sc in next ch-3 sp, (ch 3, sc in next ch-3 sp) twice, ch 1, hdc in first sc to form last sp: 110 sps.

Rnd 19: Ch 1, sc in same sp, ch 3, (dc in next dc, ch 3) 6 times, ★ skip next ch-3 sp, (sc in next ch-3 sp, ch 3) 3 times, (dc in next dc, ch 3) 6 times; repeat from ★ around to last 3 ch-3 sps, skip next ch-3 sp, sc in next ch-3 sp, ch 3, sc in next ch-3 sp, ch 1, hdc in first sc to form last sp: 99 ch-3 sps.

Rnd 20: Ch 1, sc in same sp, ch 3, dc in next dc, ch 3, (sc in next ch-3 sp, ch 3, dc in next dc, ch 3) 5 times, ★ skip next ch-3 sp, (sc in next ch-3 sp, ch 3) twice, dc in next dc, ch 3, (sc in next ch-3 sp, ch 3, dc in next dc, ch 3) 5 times; repeat from ★ around to last 2 ch-3 sps, skip next ch-3 sp, sc in last ch-3 sp, ch 1, hdc in first sc to form last sp: 143 ch-3 sps.

Rnd 21: Ch 1, sc in same sp, ch 3, dc in next dc, ch 3, (work Cluster in next ch-3 sp, ch 3) 10 times, dc in next dc, ch 3, ★ skip next ch-3 sp, sc in next ch-3 sp, ch 3, dc in next dc, ch 3, (work Cluster in next ch-3 sp, ch 3) 10 times, dc in next dc, ch 3; repeat from ★ around; join with slip st to first sc: 110 Clusters.

Rnd 22: Slip st in next ch, ch 1, (sc, ch 3, slip st in third ch from hook, sc) in same sp and in each ch-3 sp around; join with slip st to first sc, finish off.

See Washing and Blocking, page 7.

Design by Delsie Rhoades.

5. PINEAPPLE FILIGREE

Shown on page 2.

Finished Size:
10" x 18"

MATERIALS
Bedspread Weight Cotton Thread (size 10): 190 yards
Steel crochet hook, size 5 (1.90 mm) **or** size needed
for gauge

GAUGE: Through
Rnd 2 = 1⅞" x 8¾"

To work double treble crochet (abbreviated dtr), YO 3 times, insert hook in dc indicated, YO and pull up a loop (5 loops on hook), (YO and draw through 2 loops on hook) 4 times *(Figs. 8a & b, page 6)*.

Ch 59.

Foundation Rnd (Right side): Dc in fourth ch from hook **(3 skipped chs count as first dc)** and in next ch, (ch 5, skip next 3 chs, dc in next 3 chs) 9 times, ch 9; working in free loops of beginning ch *(Fig. 9, page 7)*, dc in first 3 chs, (ch 5, skip next 3 chs, dc in next 3 chs) 9 times, ch 4, dtr in first dc to form last loop: 60 dc and 20 loops.

To work Cluster (uses next 3 dc or one loop), ★ YO, insert hook in **next** st or loop indicated, YO and pull up a loop, YO and draw through 2 loops on hook; repeat from ★ 2 times **more**, YO and draw through all 4 loops on hook.

Rnd 1: Ch 1, (sc, ch 3, work Cluster, ch 3, sc) in same loop, ch 3, † work Cluster using next 3 dc, ch 3, ★ sc in next loop, ch 3, work Cluster using next 3 dc, ch 3; repeat from ★ 8 times **more** †, sc in next loop, ch 3, (work Cluster, ch 3, sc, ch 3) twice in same loop, repeat from † to † once, (sc, ch 3, work Cluster, ch 3) in same loop as first sc; join with slip st to first sc: 24 Clusters.

To work treble crochet (abbreviated tr), YO twice, insert hook in st or sp indicated, YO and pull up a loop (4 loops on hook), (YO and draw through 2 loops on hook) 3 times *(Figs. 7a & b, page 6)*.

Rnd 2: Ch 7, tr in same st, ch 3, † (dc, ch 2, dc) in next Cluster, ch 3, ★ sc in next sc, ch 3, (dc, ch 2, dc) in next Cluster, ch 3; repeat from ★ 10 times **more** †, (tr, ch 3) twice in next sc, repeat from † to † once; join with slip st to fourth ch of beginning ch-7: 48 dc and 74 sps.

Rnd 3: Slip st in next ch and in same ch-3 sp, ch 11 **(counts as first tr plus ch 7)**, † tr in next tr, ch 7, skip next ch-3 sp, tr in next ch-2 sp, ch 7, ★ skip next 2 ch-3 sps, tr in next ch-2 sp, ch 7; repeat from ★ 10 times **more**, skip next ch-3 sp, tr in next tr, ch 7 †, tr in next ch-3 sp, ch 7, repeat from † to † once; join with slip st to first tr: 30 tr and 30 loops.

To work Picot, ch 4, slip st in top of last st made.

To work beginning Shell, ch 5 **(counts as first dc plus ch 2)**, 2 dc in st or sp indicated, work Picot.

To work Shell, work (dc, Picot, dc, ch 2, 2 dc, Picot) in st or sp indicated.

Rnd 4: Work beginning Shell in same st, ch 5, sc in next tr, ch 3, 5 dc in center ch of next loop, ch 3, sc in next tr, ch 5, ★ work Shell in next tr, ch 5, sc in next tr, ch 3, 5 dc in center ch of next loop, ch 3, sc in next tr, ch 5; repeat from ★ around, dc in same st as beginning Shell, work Picot; join with slip st to first dc: 10 Shells.

Rnd 5: Slip st in first ch-2 sp, work beginning Shell in same sp, † ch 7, skip next 2 sps, 2 dc in next dc, (dc in next dc, 2 dc in next dc) twice, ch 7, work Shell in next Shell (ch-2 sp), ★ ch 5, skip next 2 sps, 2 dc in next dc, (dc in next dc, 2 dc in next dc) twice, ch 5, work Shell in next Shell; repeat from ★ 2 times more, ch 7, skip next 2 sps, 2 dc in next dc, (dc in next dc, 2 dc in next dc) twice, ch 7 †, work Shell in next Shell, repeat from † to † once, dc in same sp as beginning Shell, work Picot; join with slip st to first dc: 20 loops.

Rnd 6: Slip st in first ch-2 sp, ch 5 **(counts as first dc plus ch 2, now and throughout)**, (dc, ch 2, 2 dc, work Picot) in same sp, † ch 6, skip next loop, dc in next dc, (ch 1, dc in next dc) 7 times, ch 6, work Shell in next Shell, ★ ch 3, skip next loop, dc in next dc, (ch 1, dc in next dc) 7 times, ch 3, work Shell in next Shell; repeat from ★ 2 times **more**, ch 6, skip next loop, dc in next dc, (ch 1, dc in next dc) 7 times, ch 6 †, in next Shell work [dc, Picot, (dc, ch 2) twice, 2 dc, Picot], repeat from † to † once, dc in same sp as first dc, work Picot; join with slip st to first dc: 70 ch-1 sps and 8 Shells.

Rnd 7: Slip st in first ch-2 sp, ch 5, † (dc, ch 2) twice in next dc, 2 dc in next ch-2 sp, work Picot, ch 7, sc in next ch-1 sp, (ch 3, sc in next ch-1 sp) 6 times, ch 7, work Shell in next Shell, ★ ch 4, sc in next ch-1 sp, (ch 3, sc in next ch-1 sp) 6 times, ch 4, work Shell in next Shell; repeat from ★ 2 times **more**, ch 7, sc in next ch-1 sp, (ch 3, sc in next ch-1 sp) 6 times, ch 7 †, work (dc, Picot, dc) in next ch-2 sp, ch 2, repeat from † to † once, dc in same sp as first dc, work Picot; join with slip st to first dc: 60 ch-3 sps and 8 Shells.

Rnd 8: Slip st in first ch-2 sp, work beginning Shell in same sp, † ch 2, 3 dc in next ch-2 sp, ch 2, work Shell in next ch-2 sp, ch 7, sc in next ch-3 sp, (ch 3, sc in next ch-3 sp) 5 times, ch 7, in next Shell work (dc, Picot, dc, ch 2, dc, ch 2, 2 dc, Picot), ★ ch 4, skip next ch-4 sp, sc in next ch-3 sp, (ch 3, sc in next ch-3 sp) 5 times, ch 4, in next Shell work (dc, Picot, dc, ch 2, dc, ch 2, 2 dc, Picot); repeat from ★ 2 times **more**, ch 7, sc in next ch-3 sp, (ch 3, sc in next ch-3 sp) 5 times, ch 7 †, work Shell in next ch-2 sp, repeat from † to † once, dc in same sp as beginning Shell, work Picot; join with slip st to first dc: 50 ch-3 sps and 4 Shells.

Rnd 9: Slip st in first ch-2 sp, work beginning Shell in same sp, † ch 3, skip next 2 dc, 2 dc in each of next 3 dc, ch 3, work Shell in next Shell, ch 7, sc in next ch-3 sp, (ch 3, sc in next ch-3 sp) 4 times, ch 7, work Shell in next ch-2 sp, ch 2, work Shell in next ch-2 sp, ★ ch 4, skip next ch-4 sp, sc in next ch-3 sp, (ch 3, sc in next ch-3 sp) 4 times, ch 4, work Shell in next ch-2 sp, ch 2, work Shell in next ch-2 sp; repeat from ★ 2 times **more**, ch 7, sc in next ch-3 sp, (ch 3, sc in next ch-3 sp) 4 times, ch 7 †, work Shell in next Shell, repeat from † to † once, dc in same sp as beginning Shell, work Picot; join with slip st to first dc: 44 ch-3 sps and 20 Shells.

To work 2-dc Cluster (uses one st), ★ YO, insert hook in st indicated, YO and pull up a loop, YO and draw through 2 loops on hook; repeat from ★ once **more**, YO and draw through all 3 loops on hook.

Rnd 10: Slip st in first ch-2 sp, work beginning Shell in same sp, † ch 5, skip next 2 dc, work 2-dc Cluster in next dc, ch 1, (dc in next dc, ch 1) 4 times, work 2-dc Cluster in next dc, ch 5, work Shell in next Shell, ch 7, sc in next ch-3 sp, (ch 3, sc in next ch-3 sp) 3 times, ch 7, work Shell in next Shell, ch 2, dc in next ch-2 sp, ch 2, work Shell in next Shell, ★ ch 4, skip next ch-4 sp, sc in next ch-3 sp, (ch 3, sc in next ch-3 sp) 3 times, ch 4, work Shell in next Shell, ch 2, dc in next ch-2 sp, ch 2, work Shell in next Shell; repeat from ★ 2 times **more**, ch 7, sc in next ch-3 sp, (ch 3, sc in next ch-3 sp) 3 times, ch 7 †, work Shell in next Shell, repeat from † to † once, dc in same sp as beginning Shell, work Picot; join with slip st to first dc: 30 ch-3 sps and 20 Shells.

Rnd 11: Slip st in first ch-2 sp, work beginning Shell in same sp, † ch 5, work 2-dc Cluster in next 2-dc Cluster, ch 3, (dc in next dc, ch 3) 4 times, work 2-dc Cluster in next 2-dc Cluster, ch 5, work Shell in next Shell, ch 7, sc in next ch-3 sp, (ch 3, sc in next ch-3 sp) twice, ch 7, work Shell in next Shell, ch 5, skip next 2 dc, dc in next dc, work Picot, ch 5, work Shell in next Shell, ★ ch 4, skip next ch-4 sp, sc in next ch-3 sp, (ch 3, sc in next ch-3 sp) twice, ch 4, work Shell in next Shell, ch 5, skip next 2 dc, dc in next dc, work Picot, ch 5, work Shell in next Shell; repeat from ★ 2 times **more**, ch 7, sc in next ch-3 sp, (ch 3, sc in next ch-3 sp) twice, ch 7 †, work Shell in next Shell, repeat from † to † once, dc in same sp as beginning Shell, work Picot; join with slip st to first dc: 28 loops and 62 sps.

Rnd 12: Slip st in first ch-2 sp, work beginning Shell in same sp, † ch 6, work 2-dc Cluster in next 2-dc Cluster, ch 4, (dc in next dc, work Picot, ch 4) 4 times, work 2-dc Cluster in next 2-dc Cluster, ch 6, work Shell in next Shell, ch 7, sc in next ch-3 sp, ch 3, sc in next ch-3 sp, ch 7, work Shell in next Shell, ch 5, (dc in next loop, work Picot, ch 5) twice, work Shell in next Shell, ★ ch 4, skip next ch-4 sp, sc in next ch-3 sp, ch 3, sc in next ch-3 sp, ch 4, work Shell in next Shell, ch 5, (dc in next loop, work Picot, ch 5) twice, work Shell in next Shell; repeat from ★ 2 times **more**, ch 7, sc in next ch-3 sp, ch 3, sc in next ch-3 sp, ch 7 †, work Shell in next Shell, repeat from † to † once, dc in same sp as beginning Shell, work Picot; join with slip st to first dc: 36 loops and 52 sps.

Rnd 13: Slip st in first ch-2 sp, work beginning Shell in same sp, † ch 5, (dc in next loop, work Picot, ch 5) 7 times, work Shell in next Shell, ch 7, sc in next ch-3 sp, ch 7, work Shell in next Shell, ch 5, (dc in next loop, work Picot, ch 5) 3 times, ★ (dc, work Picot, dc, ch 2, 2 dc) in next Shell, (2 dc, ch 2, 2 dc, work Picot) in next Shell, ch 5, (dc in next loop, work Picot, ch 5) 3 times; repeat from ★ 2 times **more**, work Shell in next Shell, ch 7, sc in next ch-3 sp, ch 7 †, work Shell in next Shell, repeat from † to † once, dc in same sp as beginning Shell, work Picot; join with slip st to first dc: 56 loops and 8 Shells.

Rnd 14: Slip st in first ch-2 sp, work beginning Shell in same sp, † ch 5, (dc in next loop, work Picot, ch 5) 8 times, work Shell in next Shell, ch 7, sc in next sc, ch 7, work Shell in next Shell, ch 7, dc in next loop, work Picot, (ch 5, dc in next loop, work Picot) 3 times, ★ ch 11, skip next 2 Picots, dc in next loop, work Picot, (ch 5, dc in next loop, work Picot) 3 times; repeat from ★ 2 times **more**, ch 7, work Shell in next Shell, ch 7, sc in next sc, ch 7 †, work Shell in next Shell, repeat from † to † once, dc in same sp as beginning Shell, work Picot; join with slip st to first dc: 60 loops.

Rnd 15: Slip st in first ch-2 sp, work beginning Shell in same sp, † ch 5, (dc in next loop, work Picot, ch 5) 4 times, (dc, work Picot, ch 5) twice in center ch of next loop, (dc in next loop, work Picot, ch 5) 4 times, (work Shell in next Shell, ch 5) twice, (dc, work Picot, ch 5) twice in next loop, (dc in next loop, work Picot, ch 5) 3 times, ★ skip first 2 chs of next loop, dc in next ch, work Picot, ch 5, skip next 5 chs, dc in next ch, work Picot, ch 5, (dc in next loop, work Picot, ch 5) 3 times; repeat from ★ 2 times **more**, (dc, work Picot, ch 5) twice in next loop, work Shell in next Shell, ch 5 †, work Shell in next Shell, repeat from † to † once, dc in same sp as beginning Shell, work Picot; join with slip st to first dc: 72 loops.

Rnd 16: Slip st in first ch-2 sp, work beginning Shell in same sp, † ch 5, [(dc, work Picot, dc) in center ch of next loop, ch 5] 11 times, work Shell in next Shell, ch 3, sc in next loop, work Picot, ch 3, work Shell in next Shell, ch 5, [(dc, work Picot, dc) in center ch of next loop, ch 5] 23 times, work Shell in next Shell, ch 3, sc in next loop, work Picot, ch 3 †, work Shell in next Shell, repeat from † to † once, dc in same sp as beginning Shell, work Picot; join with slip st to first dc, finish off.

See Washing and Blocking, page 7.

Design by Lucille LaFlamme.

6. POSH PINEAPPLE

Shown on page 1.

Finished Size:
12½" diameter (point to point)

MATERIALS

Bedspread Weight Cotton Thread (size 10): 195 yards
Steel crochet hook, size 7 (1.65 mm) **or** size needed for gauge

GAUGE: Rnds 1-7 = 2½"

Ch 7; join with slip st to form a ring.

Rnd 1 (Right side)**:** Ch 3 **(counts as first dc, now and throughout)**, 23 dc in ring; join with slip st to first dc: 24 dc.

Rnd 2: Ch 1, sc in same st, ch 2, skip next dc, ★ sc in next dc, ch 2, skip next dc; repeat from ★ around; join with slip st to first sc: 12 sc and 12 ch-2 sps.

To work Front Post treble crochet (abbreviated FPtr), YO twice, insert hook from **front** to **back** around post of st indicated *(Fig. 10, page 7)*, YO and pull up a loop (4 loops on hook), (YO and draw through 2 loops on hook) 3 times.

Rnd 3: Ch 1, sc in same st, working in **front** of next ch-2, skip first dc on Rnd 1, work 2 FPtr around next dc, ★ sc in next sc on Rnd 2, working in **front** of next ch-2, skip next dc on Rnd 1, work 2 FPtr around next dc; repeat from ★ around; join with slip st to first sc: 36 sts.

To work Popcorn, 4 dc in ch-2 sp indicated, drop loop from hook, insert hook in first dc of 4-dc group, hook dropped loop and draw through.

Rnd 4: Ch 1, sc in same st, ch 3, working **behind** next 2 FPtr, work Popcorn in next ch-2 sp on Rnd 2, ch 3, ★ sc in next sc on Rnd 3, ch 3, working **behind** next 2 FPtr, work Popcorn in next ch-2 sp on Rnd 2, ch 3; repeat from ★ around; join with slip st to first sc: 24 ch-3 sps.

Rnd 5: Slip st in first ch-3 sp, ch 1, sc in same sp, ch 3, (sc in next ch-3 sp, ch 3) around; join with slip st to first sc: 24 sc and 24 ch-3 sps.

Rnd 6: Ch 1, sc in same st, 2 sc in next ch-3 sp, (sc in next sc, 2 sc in next ch-3 sp) around; join with slip st to first sc: 72 sc.

Rnd 7: Ch 1, sc in same st and in each sc around; join with slip st to first sc.

Rnd 8: Ch 5 **(counts as first dc plus ch 2, now and throughout)**, 2 dc in same st, ch 3, skip next 2 sc, sc in next sc, skip next 2 sc, dc in next sc, (ch 1, dc in same st) 4 times, skip next 2 sc, sc in next sc, ch 3, skip next 2 sc, ★ (2 dc, ch 2, 2 dc) in next sc, ch 3, skip next 2 sc, sc in next sc, skip next 2 sc, dc in next sc, (ch 1, dc in same st) 4 times, skip next 2 sc, sc in next sc, ch 3, skip next 2 sc; repeat from ★ around, dc in same st as first dc; join with slip st to first dc: 54 dc and 42 sps.

Rnd 9: Slip st in first ch-2 sp, ch 5, 2 dc in same sp, ch 2, sc in next ch-3 sp, skip next sc, dc in next dc, (dc in next ch-1 sp and in next dc) 4 times, sc in next ch-3 sp, ch 2, ★ (2 dc, ch 2) twice in next ch-2 sp, sc in next ch-3 sp, skip next sc, dc in next dc, (dc in next ch-1 sp and in next dc) 4 times, sc in next ch-3 sp, ch 2; repeat from ★ around, dc in same sp as first dc; join with slip st to first dc: 78 dc and 18 ch-2 sps.

Rnd 10: Slip st in first ch-2 sp, ch 5, 2 dc in same sp, ch 2, sc in next ch-2 sp, skip next sc, dc in next dc, (ch 1, dc in next dc) 8 times, sc in next ch-2 sp, ch 2, ★ (2 dc, ch 2) twice in next ch-2 sp, sc in next ch-2 sp, skip next sc, dc in next dc, (ch 1, dc in next dc) 8 times, sc in next ch-2 sp, ch 2; repeat from ★ around, dc in same sp as first dc; join with slip st to first dc: 66 sps.

To work dc Cluster (uses one sp), ★ YO, insert hook in sp indicated, YO and pull up a loop, YO and draw through 2 loops on hook; repeat from ★ 2 times **more**, YO and draw through all 4 loops on hook.

Rnd 11: Slip st in first ch-2 sp, ch 5, 2 dc in same sp, ch 2, sc in next ch-2 sp, work dc Cluster in next ch-1 sp, (ch 2, work dc Cluster in next ch-1 sp) 7 times, sc in next ch-2 sp, ch 2, ★ (2 dc, ch 2) twice in next ch-2 sp, sc in next ch-2 sp, work dc Cluster in next ch-1 sp, (ch 2, work dc Cluster in next ch-1 sp) 7 times, sc in next ch-2 sp, ch 2; repeat from ★ around, dc in same sp as first dc; join with slip st to first dc: 60 ch-2 sps.

Rnd 12: Slip st in first ch-2 sp, ch 5, 2 dc in same sp, ch 2, sc in next ch-2 sp, ch 1, work dc Cluster in next ch-2 sp, (ch 2, work dc Cluster in next ch-2 sp) 6 times, ch 1, sc in next ch-2 sp, ch 2, ★ (2 dc, ch 2) twice in next ch-2 sp, sc in next ch-2 sp, ch 1, work dc Cluster in next ch-2 sp, (ch 2, work dc Cluster in next ch-2 sp) 6 times, ch 1, sc in next ch-2 sp, ch 2; repeat from ★ around, dc in same sp as first dc; join with slip st to first dc: 66 sps.

Rnd 13: Slip st in first ch-2 sp, ch 5, 2 dc in same sp, ch 2, ★ † 2 sc in next ch-2 sp, sc in next ch-1 sp, ch 2, (work dc Cluster in next ch-2 sp, ch 2) 6 times, sc in next ch-1 sp, 2 sc in next ch-2 sp, ch 2 †, (2 dc, ch 2) 3 times in next ch-2 sp; repeat from ★ 4 times **more**, then repeat from † to † once, (2 dc, ch 2, dc) in same sp as first dc; join with slip st to first dc.

To work decrease *(uses next 2 ch-2 sps),* ★ YO, insert hook in **next** ch-2 sp, YO and pull up a loop, YO and draw through 2 loops on hook; repeat from ★ once **more**, YO and draw through all 3 loops on hook.

Rnd 14: Slip st in first ch-2 sp, ch 5, 2 dc in same sp, ★ † ch 1, decrease, ch 4, work dc Cluster in next ch-2 sp, (ch 2, work dc Cluster in next ch-2 sp) 4 times, ch 4, decrease, ch 1, (2 dc, ch 2, 2 dc) in next ch-2 sp, ch 4 †, (2 dc, ch 2, 2 dc) in next ch-2 sp; repeat from ★ 4 times **more**, then repeat from † to † once, dc in same sp as first dc; join with slip st to first dc.

Rnd 15: Slip st in first ch-2 sp, ch 5, 2 dc in same sp, ★ † ch 1, skip next ch-1 sp, sc in next ch-4 sp, ch 3, work dc Cluster in next ch-2 sp, (ch 2, work dc Cluster in next ch-2 sp) 3 times, ch 3, sc in next ch-4 sp, ch 1, skip next ch-1 sp, (2 dc, ch 2, 2 dc) in next ch-2 sp, ch 3, (dc, ch 5, dc) in next ch-4 sp, ch 3 †, (2 dc, ch 2, 2 dc) in next ch-2 sp; repeat from ★ 4 times **more**, then repeat from † to † once, dc in same sp as first dc; join with slip st to first dc: 72 sps.

To work treble crochet *(abbreviated tr),* YO twice, insert hook in st or sp indicated, YO and pull up a loop (4 loops on hook), (YO and draw through 2 loops on hook) 3 times **(Figs. 7a & b, page 6)**.

Rnd 16: Slip st in first ch-2 sp, ch 5, 2 dc in same sp, ★ † ch 1, skip next ch-1 sp, sc in next ch-3 sp, ch 3, work dc Cluster in next ch-2 sp, (ch 2, work dc Cluster in next ch-2 sp) twice, ch 3, sc in next ch-3 sp, ch 1, skip next ch-1 sp, (2 dc, ch 2, 2 dc) in next ch-2 sp, ch 3, skip next ch-3 sp, tr in next dc, ch 1, (tr, ch 1) 7 times in next ch-5 sp, tr in next dc, ch 3, skip next ch-3 sp †, (2 dc, ch 2, 2 dc) in next ch-2 sp; repeat from ★ 4 times **more**, then repeat from † to † once, dc in same sp as first dc; join with slip st to first dc: 108 sps.

Rnd 17: Slip st in first ch-2 sp, ch 5, 2 dc in same sp, ★ † ch 1, skip next ch-1 sp, sc in next ch-3 sp, ch 3, work dc Cluster in next ch-2 sp, ch 2, work dc Cluster in next ch-2 sp, ch 3, sc in next ch-3 sp, ch 1, skip next ch-1 sp, (2 dc, ch 2, 2 dc) in next ch-2 sp, ch 3, sc in next ch-3 sp, ch 2, (work dc Cluster in next ch-1 sp, ch 2) 8 times, sc in next ch-3 sp, ch 3 †, (2 dc, ch 2, 2 dc) in next ch-2 sp; repeat from ★ 4 times **more**, then repeat from † to † once, dc in same sp as first dc; join with slip st to first dc.

Rnd 18: Slip st in first ch-2 sp, ch 5, 2 dc in same sp, ★ † ch 1, skip next ch-1 sp, sc in next ch-3 sp, ch 3, work dc Cluster in next ch-2 sp, ch 3, sc in next ch-3 sp, ch 1, skip next ch-1 sp, (2 dc, ch 2, 2 dc) in next ch-2 sp, ch 3, 2 sc in next ch-3 sp, sc in next ch-2 sp, (sc, ch 3, sc) in next 7 ch-2 sps, sc in next ch-2 sp, 2 sc in next ch-3 sp, ch 3 †, (2 dc, ch 2, 2 dc) in next ch-2 sp; repeat from ★ 4 times **more**, then repeat from † to † once, dc in same sp as first dc; join with slip st to first dc: 90 sps.

Rnd 19: Slip st in first ch-2 sp, ch 5, 2 dc in same sp, ★ † ch 1, skip next ch-1 sp, sc in next ch-3 sp, ch 5, sc in next ch-3 sp, ch 1, skip next ch-1 sp, (2 dc, ch 2, 2 dc) in next ch-2 sp, ch 3, 2 sc in next ch-3 sp, dc in next ch-3 sp, (ch 1, dc in same sp) 3 times, [sc in next ch-3 sp, dc in next ch-3 sp, (ch 1, dc in same sp) 3 times] 3 times, 2 sc in next ch-3 sp, ch 3 †, (2 dc, ch 2, 2 dc) in next ch-2 sp; repeat from ★ 4 times **more**, then repeat from † to † once, dc in same sp as first dc; join with slip st to first dc: 114 sps.

Rnd 20: Slip st in first ch-2 sp, ch 3, dc in same sp, ★ † skip next ch-1 sp, sc in next ch-5 sp, skip next ch-1 sp, 2 dc in next ch-2 sp, ch 4, 3 sc in next ch-3 sp, sc in next 2 ch-1 sps, ch 1, skip next 2 dc, (dc, ch 1) 4 times in next sc, skip next ch-1 sp, [sc in next ch-1 sp, ch 1, skip next 2 dc, (dc, ch 1) 4 times in next sc, skip next ch-1 sp] 2 times, sc in next 2 ch-1 sps, 3 sc in next ch-3 sp, ch 4 †, 2 dc in next ch-2 sp; repeat from ★ 4 times **more**, then repeat from † to † once; join with slip st to first dc: 102 sps.

To work beginning Split Cluster *(uses next 4 sts)*, ch 2, † YO, insert hook in **next** dc, YO and pull up a loop, YO and draw through 2 loops on hook †, YO, skip next sc, insert hook in next dc, YO and pull up a loop (4 loops on hook), YO and draw through 2 loops on hook, repeat from † to † once, YO and draw through all 4 loops on hook.

To work Split Cluster *(uses next 5 sts)*, † YO, insert hook in **next** dc, YO and pull up a loop, YO and draw through 2 loops on hook †, repeat from † to † once **more**, YO, skip next sc, insert hook in next dc, YO and pull up a loop (5 loops on hook), YO and draw through 2 loops on hook, repeat from † to † once, YO and draw through all 5 loops on hook.

Rnd 21: Work beginning Split Cluster, ★ † ch 4, 3 sc in next ch-4 sp, ch 5, sc in next 3 ch-1 sps, ch 1, skip next 2 dc, (dc, ch 1) 6 times in next sc, skip next 2 ch-1 sps, sc in next ch-1 sp, ch 1, skip next 2 dc, (dc, ch 1) 6 times in next sc, skip next 2 ch-1 sps, sc in next 3 ch-1 sps, ch 5, 3 sc in next ch-4 sp, ch 4 †, work Split Cluster; repeat from ★ 4 times **more**, then repeat from † to † once; join with slip st to top of beginning Split Cluster: 108 sps.

Rnd 22: Slip st in first ch-4 sp, ch 1, (sc, ch 4) twice in same sp and in next ch-5 sp, ★ † sc in next 4 ch-1 sps, ch 1, skip next 3 dc, (tr, ch 1) 6 times in next sc, skip next 3 ch-1 sps, sc in next 4 ch-1 sps, (ch 4, sc) twice in next 2 sps †, (sc, ch 4) twice in next 2 sps; repeat from ★ 4 times **more**, then repeat from † to † once; join with slip st to first sc: 132 sts and 90 sps.

To work Small Picot, ch 2, slip st in top of last sc made.

Rnd 23: Ch 1, sc in same st and in next ch-4 sp, ★ † ch 5, sc in next ch-4 sp, work dc Cluster in next ch-4 sp, (ch 3, work dc Cluster in same sp) twice, 2 sc in next ch-4 sp, sc in next 4 sc, (sc in next ch-1 sp and in next tr) 3 times, 3 sc in next ch-1 sp, (sc in next tr and in next ch-1 sp) 3 times, sc in next 4 sc, 2 sc in next ch-4 sp, work dc Cluster in next ch-4 sp, (ch 3, work dc Cluster in same sp) twice, sc in next ch-4 sp, ch 5, sc in next ch-4 sp and in next sc, work Small Picot †, sc in next sc and in next ch-4 sp; repeat from ★ 4 times **more**, then repeat from † to † once; join with slip st to first sc: 198 sc and 36 sps.

To work tr Cluster, ch 3, ★ YO twice, insert hook in top of last sc made, YO and pull up a loop, (YO and draw through 2 loops on hook) twice; repeat from ★ once **more**, YO and draw through all 3 loops on hook.

To work Large Picot, ch 3, slip st in top of last sc made.

Rnd 24: Slip st in next sc and in next ch-5 sp, ch 1, 5 sc in same sp, ★ † 3 sc in next ch-3 sp, (sc, work Large Picot, sc) in next dc Cluster, 3 sc in next ch-3 sp, skip next dc Cluster, sc in next sc, (ch 1, slip st in top of sc just made, sc in next sc) 9 times, work tr Cluster, skip next 3 sc, (sc, work Large Picot, sc) in next sc, work tr Cluster, skip next 3 sc, sc in next sc, (ch 1, slip st in top of sc just made, sc in next sc) 9 times, 3 sc in next ch-3 sp, (sc, work Large Picot, sc) in next dc Cluster, 3 sc in next ch-3 sp, 5 sc in next ch-5 sp, ch 4, slip st in third ch from hook, ch 2 †, 5 sc in next ch-5 sp; repeat from ★ 4 times **more**, then repeat from † to † once; join with slip st to first sc, finish off.

See Washing and Blocking, page 7.

Design by Patricia Kristoffersen.

4